Remembering
Ann Arbor

Alice Goff and Megan Cooney

TRADE PAPER PRESS

Panorama of Ann Arbor from Sunset Road (formerly Chubb Road) facing southeast, circa 1890.

Remembering
Ann Arbor

Turner Publishing Company
200 4th Avenue North • Suite 950
Nashville, Tennessee 37219
(615) 255-2665

Remembering Ann Arbor

www.turnerpublishing.com

Library of Congress Control Number: 2010924312

ISBN: 978-1-59652-655-6

Printed in the United States of America

10 11 12 13 14 15 16—0 9 8 7 6 5 4 3 2 1

CONTENTS

A Navy recruiting officer and couple. Military recruiting was especially vigorous in Ann Arbor, with its high population of young people. In 1942, the University Regents established the Division for Emergency Training, aimed at students preparing for military service.

Acknowledgments

This volume, *Remembering Ann Arbor,* is the result of the cooperation and efforts of many individuals and organizations. It is with great thanks that we acknowledge in particular the Bentley Historical Library, University of Michigan, for their generous support.

The writers would also like to thank Karen Jania and the Bentley Historical Library reference staff for all of their help and support.

PREFACE

Ann Arbor has thousands of historic photographs that reside in archives, both locally and nationally. This book began with the observation that, while those photographs are of great interest to many, they are not easily accessible. During a time when Ann Arbor is looking ahead and evaluating its future course, many people are asking, How do we treat the past? These decisions affect every aspect of the city—architecture, public spaces, commerce, infrastructure—and these, in turn, affect the way that people live their lives. This book seeks to provide easy access to a valuable, objective look into the history of Ann Arbor.

The power of photographs is that they are less subjective than words in their treatment of history. Although the photographer can make subjective decisions regarding subject matter and how to capture and present it, photographs seldom interpret the past to the extent textual histories can. For this reason, photography is uniquely positioned to offer an original, untainted look at the past, allowing the viewer to learn for himself what the world was like a century or more ago.

This project represents countless hours of review and research. The researchers and writers have reviewed thousands of photographs in numerous archives. We greatly appreciate the generous assistance of the individuals and organizations listed in the acknowledgments of this work, without whom this project could not have been completed.

The goal in publishing this work is to provide broader access to this set of extraordinary photographs that seek to inspire, provide perspective, and evoke insight that might assist people who are responsible for determining Ann Arbor's future. In addition, the book seeks to preserve the past with adequate respect and reverence.

With the exception of touching up imperfections that have accrued with the passage of time and cropping where necessary, no changes have been made. The focus and clarity of many images are limited to the technology and the ability of the photographer at the time they were recorded.

The work is divided into eras. Beginning with some of the earliest known photographs of Ann Arbor, the first section records photographs through the end of the nineteenth century. The second section spans the beginning of the twentieth century through World War I. Section Three looks at the years between 1920 and 1960.

In each of these sections we have made an effort to capture various aspects of life through our selection of photographs. People, commerce, transportation, infrastructure, religious institutions, and educational institutions have been included to provide a broad perspective.

We encourage readers to reflect as they go walking in Ann Arbor, strolling through the city, its parks, and its neighborhoods. It is the publisher's hope that in utilizing this work, longtime residents will learn something new and that new residents will gain a perspective on where Ann Arbor has been, so that each can contribute to its future.

—Todd Bottorff, Publisher

Located on the southwest corner of Main and Washington streets, the Hangsterfer Block (building) was erected in 1860 by German immigrant Jacob Hangsterfer. The First National Bank opened on the ground floor in 1863, joining Hangsterfer's confectionery. The third floor was a large ballroom (known as Hangsterfer Hall) that served as an important cultural center for many years, hosting popular dances, plays, and social gatherings.

Growth of a University Town

(1860s–1899)

The Gregory House, circa 1868. Located on the northwest corner of Huron and Main streets, the Gregory replaced the American Hotel in 1862. By 1872, Ann Arbor had eight hotels.

A view of Main Street northwest from Washington Street, circa 1871-74. The Gregory House is visible at the corner of Huron and Main, and toward the foreground, Hutzel & Company's storefront advertises paints and oils.

First Presbyterian Church, at Huron and Division streets, ca. 1865. Built in 1860, this structure housed the church until the congregation moved to their current location, on the eastern side of town on Washtenaw Avenue. In 1935 the building was demolished. The Ann Arbor News building is now located on the site.

The Danforth and Royce houses at the corner of Ann Street and Fifth Avenue, circa 1875. Attorney George Danforth built his Greek Revival home on this corner in 1845. The cabinetmaker James F. Royce then built his Italianate house next door in 1866, after coming to Ann Arbor in 1830 and operating a chair-making business for several decades. Royce's house still stands, though it is currently rented as apartments.

Ann Arbor's volunteer fire department, shown here in 1877, was organized in 1838 and replaced by a paid crew in 1888.

Drake's saloon and Jacob Haller's Jewelry on East Huron Street, circa 1875. These shops were located in the thriving commercial district across the street from Ann Arbor's courthouse. Haller's Jewelry was established in 1858 and operated continuously for more than one hundred years.

State Street facing north, from North University, circa 1877. Visible here is the spire of the Methodist Church, at State and Washington, and the front of Sheehan's bookstore, which was the first of many bookstores in this area. University scholars (wearing mortarboards) linger on the street.

A view of the Huron River, facing east, circa 1870. The area north of the river was still very rural at this time. The old Wall Street Bridge is visible in the distance.

A beer delivery wagon in front of Binder's Saloon in 1872. Binder's saloon was located at 112 West Liberty, an area home to a number of German businesses. By 1872, there were 49 saloons in Ann Arbor, up from 10 in 1860.

The John Nickels Meat Market, on State Street at North University, circa 1870s. John Nickels operated this market from his home—he and his family lived in the back of the building. In 1915, the Nickels family built the Nickels Arcade on the same spot. The building at right housed a dining hall for students.

First German Church in Michigan, in 1881. In 1833, Pastor Friedrich Schmid founded this church for Ann Arbor's German immigrant population, who wanted to hear sermons in their native language. The church was located on the western side of town on Jackson Road, where Bethlehem Cemetery is today.

Ann Arbor from the northwest, in 1876. The 1866 Methodist Church can be seen to the left of the dome of University Hall, both visible on the skyline.

The Ann Arbor Organ Works, at the northwest corner of First and Washington streets, circa 1872. The company was founded in 1872 by David F. Allmendinger, and originally located in these buildings, where he lived with his family. Eventually, the buildings in this complex were demolished to make way for large, brick factory buildings, where Allmendinger built not only organs, but also pianos. The brick buildings still stand today, taking up the entire block on First Street between Huron and Washington.

Shown here around 1885, this wooden railroad trestle was replaced with a steel one in 1891, which subsequently collapsed in 1904.

The Second Courthouse was built in 1878 and occupied the entire block bounded by Huron, Main, Ann, and Fourth streets. It was set in the center of the block and surrounded by grass and shade trees. This building replaced the first courthouse, built in 1834 on the same block, facing south from Ann Street, with a large public square at its front.

A seventh-grade class picture, June 14, 1884. In 1884, there were five public ward schools for the younger children of Ann Arbor.

This icehouse was located on the Huron River, near Argo Pond. Harvested ice was stored near the river in icehouses like this one, and delivered during the warm weather months to businesses and private homes for use in iceboxes.

Ann Arbor Central Mills, South First Street between Liberty and Washington, circa 1882. From the 1850s through the 1870s, this location housed various breweries—it was ideal for its proximity to the cool waters of Allen Creek, as well as to the roads leading out of Ann Arbor. In 1882, the building was purchased by the Ann Arbor Central Mills, a successful flour mill well into the twentieth century. Around 1900 the clapboard building shown here was replaced with a brick building, which still stands today.

A skating party made up of men and boys poses with their dog. Skating on the Huron River and on local ponds was a popular cold-weather activity.

The Germania Club, circa 1885. By 1880, Americans of German ethnicity made up nearly 50 percent of Ann Arbor's total population, forming many social organizations. This club often held meetings on the top floor of Michael Staebler's Germania Hotel.

The view from University Hall, facing north, circa 1880. This image provides a glimpse of the expanding Ann Arbor skyline, with the 1866 Methodist church on State and Washington clearly visible on the left and the arched windows on Union High School (later Ann Arbor High School) toward the right. In the foreground is the Law building.

The heating plant for the University of Michigan, circa 1883-84. This plant, located where the Randall Laboratory Building is today, provided heat for the Engineering Building, the Engineering shops, and the Physics Laboratory. It was demolished in 1894 to make way for the university's first central heating plant, which was built on the same location.

A view of State Street from North University, circa 1880. Here are the beginnings of the development of the commercial area on State Street: Sheehan & Co.'s bookstore is located at center, and a building advertising a skating rink is to its left.

The Germania Hotel and Heinzman & Son's Harness Shop, at 117-123 West Washington, circa 1885-90. Michael Staebler was a German immigrant who moved to Ann Arbor in 1885 and built the Germania Hotel, eventually renaming it the American Hotel. Staebler sold coal from his storefront on the right, later selling bicycles out of the same shop. He was also the first in town to sell automobiles, in 1900.

The Men's Bicycle Club poses with penny-farthings on the courthouse steps in 1887. Junius Beal, publisher and editor of the *Ann Arbor Courier* and later a University of Michigan regent, straddles his penny-farthing at far-right.

The Bach & Abel Dry Goods Store, at the corner of Main and Washington streets, in 1886. Shown here are the employees of Bach & Abel, as well as some of their merchandise, which has been displayed on the plank sidewalk. Philip Bach himself can be seen here on the right, and his partner, Eugene Abel, is the gentleman standing fourth from left. In 1895, Bach's store was purchased by Bruno St. James, whose bookkeeper, Bertha Muehlig, later owned and ran the dry goods business here from 1911 until her death in 1955.

G. H. Wild's Tailor Shop, at 108 E. Washington, circa 1890s. Gottlieb H. Wild operated his tailor shop here at the end of the nineteenth century, advertising himself as "the leading tailor for fine dress suits" in the 1894 City Directory.

A gentleman crosses Main Street, sometime after 1890. The sign for public baths on the west side of the street indicates that although the city had running water beginning in 1885, not all of the townspeople were able to take advantage of it right away.

Ann Arbor newsboys in 1892. A wide array of newspapers were available for the discerning Ann Arbor reader in that year, some of which may have been hawked by youngsters like these young men in Courthouse Square. The *Ann Arbor Argus* was a Democratic rag, advertised as the oldest paper in town, and the *Ann Arbor Courier* was its Republican rival. There were also two newspapers for German immigrants and a number of other politically themed choices.

Trinity Lutheran Church, circa 1896. The church was founded in 1893, and this structure, on the corner of William Street and 5th Avenue, was dedicated on April 5, 1896. Trinity was the first English-language Methodist church in town (all other Methodist services were given in German). When the land was sold to the Y.M.C.A. in 1956 and the building demolished, the congregation moved to their current location on West Stadium Boulevard.

The Main Post Office, at the northeast corner of Main and Ann streets. Also known as the Beal Block, this building was constructed in 1882 by publisher Rice Beal. It served as the post office from 1882 to 1909, and was a local gathering place for townspeople, who retrieved their own mail here before home delivery began in 1886. The building was demolished in 1935.

The scene on State Street, sometime in 1893. George Wahr's bookstore at 316 S. State Street advertises textbooks at the lowest prices.

Island Park was established in the 1890s as one of Ann Arbor's first real parks. Public events, such as the Fourth of July concert given here annually by Otto's Band, added to its immense popularity.

A Weinmann & Hoelzle parade float. Like most Americans, the citizens of Ann Arbor loved a parade, and parades provided an excellent opportunity for local businesses to advertise their goods.

Postal Telegraph Cable Company operators in the Cornwell (Hamilton) Building at East Huron and North Fourth, in the mid-1890s. This was one of many telegraph offices that once faced Courthouse Square.

In 1881, Mack & Company's department store was the first local business to replace wooden sidewalks with stone slabs. As other stores and then residents followed suit, the demand for marble increased. Seen here are marble slabs being offloaded from the railroad, sometime after 1890.

Wahr & Miller, at 218 S. Main Street, circa 1899, offered all the latest in fall and winter shoe styles.

Here around the 1890s, the patriotic bunting decorating the buildings and the presence of a float suggests that a parade is in progress. Any reason to organize a parade was sufficient—from principal holidays to local developments. In 1883, the volunteer fire department celebrated their acquisition of a new hose cart with an impromptu parade through the streets, accompanied by a brass band.

Cleaning wooden sidewalks on South State Street, before 1893. The introduction of postal collection boxes limited the need for students and townspeople living near the university to travel to the downtown post office, further hastening the commercial development of the State Street area.

The Central Railroad Depot. Built in 1886, this train station was considered to be the finest on the Michigan Central line. The interior was as ornate as the exterior, featuring terra-cotta fireplaces and stained-glass windows. Travelers coming into Ann Arbor could expect to be greeted by throngs of people in the station, and by horse-drawn carriages lining the street beyond to take them to their destination. This building is now home to the Gandy Dancer restaurant.

State Street, in 1892. By this time a multitude of bookstores lined State Street, much as they do now.

In 1898, employees of the Hutzel & Company hardware store and plumbing firm demonstrate some new items—useful thanks to the installation of running water and a sanitary sewer system. The items on this parade float include flush toilets and claw-foot bathtubs.

Railway passengers wait for the train to clear the Broadway Bridge, circa 1890s.

The "Diag," at the corner of State and North University, after 1890. As evidenced by the sign at the entrance to campus, the sale of University of Michigan souvenirs was already a popular commercial pursuit.

The Ann Arbor Organ Company, at the southeast corner of Main and Liberty streets, in 1893. The organs and pianos that were made in David Allmendinger's factory were sold here in his retail store.

A derailment at Miller Avenue in 1893. Disasters such as fires and train derailments often brought out the whole town. Here a few curious townspeople and children approach the stranded steam engine.

A parade on Main Street, circa 1898–1900. For decades after its construction, the courthouse remained a focal point of the town, and any parade would necessarily pass right in front of it. On the corner of Main and Ann streets is the main Post Office. The streets are now paved, but it is clear that just a few blocks north, Main Street remains undeveloped.

Seen here in 1895, this float, decorated with apples, has presumably stopped on its way to join a harvest-themed parade. Visible behind the float is the Buchoz Block, located at Detroit Street. On the far right is the Half Way Saloon, whose name referred to the location of the block on the trolley line, halfway between the railroad depot and downtown.

An important citizen seems to be riding in his carriage in this 1897 parade, doffing his hat to the assembled crowd. A concession stand sells hot sausage and soft drinks in the background.

Two conductors pose in front of a Packard-Huron streetcar, circa 1890s. Ann Arbor's streetcar line operated from 1890 until 1924, when, with much fanfare, the old cars were replaced with buses.

The old University Library, circa 1890s. The first library building, built in 1883, served not only as a library, but also as an art gallery. When it was replaced with the Harlan Hatcher Library in 1920, architects chose to build around the older structure, with the result that the first library's stacks are still in use.

First Baptist Church, at Huron Street between Division and State, late in the nineteenth century. The First Baptist Church was founded in 1828, and spent its early years frequently changing locations. The congregation was located in Lower Town from 1832 to 1849, then on Catherine Street until 1881, when its current home (shown here) was completed.

Ann Arbor's Company A, First Infantry, Michigan National Guard, 1898. The Company posed on the courthouse steps for a formal portrait before leaving for the Spanish-American War. This group of volunteer soldiers was headed for Cuba.

Automobiles, War, and Influenza

(1900–1919)

A daring fellow straddles a telephone pole above State Street, ca. 1900. Although the first telephone exchange in Ann Arbor was established in 1881, the service was very expensive. For many years, only businesses and a limited number of wealthy townspeople could afford to have their own lines installed. In 1897, a second private company with cheaper rates established service in the area and forced down prices, making it easier for townspeople to afford telephones.

Main Street, facing north from Liberty Street, circa 1908. In the foreground is Mack and Company, Ann Arbor's largest department store. By 1908, Main Street was fully paved (brick paving was installed in 1898), and townspeople wishing to do their shopping could travel streets that were dust-free, by trolley or horse-drawn carriage.

The Michigan Beef & Provision Company at 140 South State Street, in the early 1900s. Stone sidewalks had been installed by this time, but refrigeration was still many years away.

A flotilla of canoes on the Huron River, probably early 1900s. The occupants are all gazing toward the canoes at center-right, where a contest of some kind seems to be in progress.

Man with a bicycle, circa 1900. With the invention of pneumatic tires, riding a bicycle became much more comfortable, and therefore even more popular in Ann Arbor.

The Savings Bank Block, northwest corner of Main and Huron, circa 1905. The Ann Arbor Savings Bank was organized in 1869, making it the third-oldest bank in Ann Arbor. This building previously housed the Gregory Hotel.

Around 1910, this bar featured not only electric light fixtures, but also an electric ceiling fan.

This steel railroad trestle installed in 1891 replaced the earlier wooden trestle, but it was too weak for heavier trains and collapsed in 1904.

The Brotherhood of Painters and Decorators float is shown on North Ashley Street in 1901 during "the biggest parade Ann Arbor ever seen," as it was described on the back of the original photograph. The occasion of that parade was not explained.

The Ann Arbor Central Mills, circa 1900. This building, located on South First Street between Liberty and Washington, replaced the clapboard structure that previously housed the Central Mills. The northernmost building in this compound was built for use as mill offices, and now houses the Blind Pig, a popular nightclub and music venue.

Main Street, facing southeast from Huron, in 1907. At left, Goodyear's Drugstore offers physicians' supplies.

Aftermath of the Argo Mills Fire of 1904. The mills, located on the northern side of the Huron River at Broadway, burned down that January. The Michigan Milling Company, its owner, then built the Argo Powerhouse on this site to power its other mills. The facility was purchased by the Eastern Michigan Edison Company in 1905.

Hose Company No. 3 leaves the engine house for a fire in 1906. The firehouse was designed by Detroit architect William Scott in the Italian villa–style and built in 1882-83. Today this building houses the Ann Arbor Hands-On Museum.

The West End Rifle Team practices their marksmanship in Schuetzenbund ("Shooting Team") Park, now Fritz Park, on Pauline Boulevard, circa 1910.

Main Street, facing south from Huron, in 1910. Every kind of transportation available to townspeople of the time is visible here, except automobiles, which hadn't yet grown popular. There are horse-drawn carriages, a streetcar, bicycles, and people on foot. By 1908, although more than 15,000 people called the city home, only 40 automobiles plied city streets.

This image was used to advertise Michigan Union's county fair for 1908. The Michigan Union was an organization of male students founded in 1904 to coordinate and maintain a student union. They sponsored a variety of social events, including the popular Union Opera, and activities such as this county fair.

The Ann Arbor Police Department in 1908. Organized in 1871, the department fulfilled the wishes of the townspeople by attempting to control the rowdy behavior of students and warn of fires. Previously, the city's law enforcement duties had been assigned to a part-time marshal and ward constables.

A boat livery, circa 1901-16. Located on the Huron River at North Main Street, this private company rented boats to University of Michigan students and visitors. Boating and canoeing on the Huron River continues to be a popular recreational activity.

View of a train accident on the Ann Arbor Railroad in 1908. The wreck took place just north of the depot at 416 South Ashley Street. The Ann Arbor Railroad operated between Toledo, Ohio, and Frankfort, Michigan, bringing supplies to town and ferrying townspeople on short-distance trips.

A Michigan Union circus parade in 1909. This procession, an example of the social activities organized by the Michigan Union Club, marched south on State Street, attracting the attention of curious children. The First Congregational Church, founded in 1876, can be seen behind the crowd on the corner of State and William streets.

The Ann Arbor High School football squad practices at the fairgrounds in 1908. The area reserved for the county fairgrounds in 1908 is now the site of Burns Park.

A delivery wagon at Fischer & Finnell's Cigar Company, South State Street at Packard, before 1910. This store served as an interurban stop, until the service ended in 1929. It still stands today and continues to be part of an important shopping district for students living south of campus.

Huron Street, facing east from Main Street, in 1907. Opened in 1883, the Farmers and Mechanics Bank, on the corner, was partly demolished by a crash of the interurban in 1927. Bicycles had gained in popularity by this time, as evidenced by their presence on the street.

A Walker Livery cutter in 1910. Winter travel was easier by cutter than by buggy, especially in rural areas where snow removal was difficult.

Hose Company No. 1, Ann Arbor Fire Department, 1906. In spite of a number of particularly devastating fires, including the Argo Mills fire of 1904, the townspeople of Ann Arbor repeatedly voted down proposals for the fire department to switch to motorized fire engines. Finally, in 1915 a fire truck was procured for the department and the old horse-drawn engines were gradually phased out.

The Michigan Union advertises a minstrel show circa 1910. In 1907, the student union had raised enough money to purchase the home of faculty member Thomas M. Cooley on State Street to use as its headquarters. In 1916, construction began on a new Michigan Union building, located on the same site.

Huron Street and Fourth Avenue, facing east, circa 1910s. The building across the street from the Cook House Hotel is the Hamilton Block (later known as the Cornwell building), built in 1882. It housed the Postal Telegraph Cable Company on its first floor in the 1890s and a bowling alley at the time of the photograph. Visible down the street is the firehouse.

Construction of Barton Dam is under way in 1912. Barton Dam was the first of four dams constructed on the Huron River by Detroit Edison (along with its subsidiary, Eastern Michigan Edison Company) to supply the city with more hydroelectric power. The dam was designed by Professor Emil Lorch, head of the University of Michigan School of Architecture.

Otto's Band marches west on North University Avenue, east of State Street, in 1914. The Otto family was responsible for much of the music played at city gatherings and parades for the last part of the nineteenth century and the first part of the twentieth. Henry Otto was the conductor and leader of the band in the 1870s and 1880s, and his son Louis took over in the 1890s, continuing the tradition until after World War I.

East Liberty Street circa 1910. On the left streetcorner stands Allmendinger Music Shop. Allmendinger remained a big name in Ann Arbor commerce. By 1906, the manufacturer was producing 300 organs and 50 pianos a month.

A Merchant's Delivery Company horse-drawn wagon in 1911. At this time horse-drawn vehicles were still prevalent, but most companies would switch to automobiles in the coming years.

The Fischer and Finnell Cigar Store in 1910.

The staff of B. St. James Dry Goods and Notions, at 126 South Main Street, in 1909. The woman standing third from right is Bertha Muehlig, then the store's bookkeeper. Two years later, Muehlig would buy the store, renaming it Muehlig's. A 1924 history of the city said that "she is a native of Ann Arbor, and one of which the city can be proud."

The first automobile arrived in Ann Arbor in 1901. By 1927, one in every five citizens owned a car.

Idlers pass the time beside the Huron River in 1910. Behind them, ads for Owl cigars and Staebler & Wuerth clothiers and furnishers decorate the building beyond the bridge.

Motor Car no. 1 ran on gasoline, on a route from Ann Arbor to Whitmore Lake in the 1910s.

The Central Flyer, circa 1910.

Circus animals are offloaded from the train at Michigan Central Station in 1913.

The Barnum and Bailey Circus was a popular attraction in many towns throughout the country. Until the 1930s, circus workers would camp out in Burns Park during their stay in Ann Arbor.

A rooftop view of town from the courthouse, facing southeast.

By the 1910s the University of Michigan had converted to the automobile. The university relied mainly on utility vehicles, like this truck, for various campus maintenance tasks.

An early biplane prepares for take-off in 1910.

A rooftop view from the courthouse, facing north. The new Ann Arbor Times-News building stands in the foreground on Ann Street. The *Times News* was formed in 1908 out of a merger between the two local papers, the *Ann Arbor News* and the *Daily Times*. The *Times-News* was very well connected. By the early 1920s, the paper had, unusually, both a Morse and an automatic telegraph wire running into the offices.

A 1925 history of Ann Arbor praised the city's schools: "Because Ann Arbor is the seat of one of the country's largest universities, something out of the ordinary might reasonably be expected of the public school system of that city. One has to live but a short time in Ann Arbor to know that this expectation has been realized." Miss Lily E. Goodhew and her class pose for a photograph at the Donovan School in 1911.

Long a symbol of local civic pride, the 1882 fire station continues to stand at Huron Street and N. 5th Avenue in its original form with no significant structural alterations. It was listed on the National Register of Historic Places in 1972.

A Cousins & Hall Florists delivery truck. The company had its own greenhouses on the corner of South University and Haven Street, now the location of the School of Education.

The Huron River is the largest waterway in Ann Arbor and flows to the southeast through town toward Ypsilanti from its origin in Oakland County.

The Merchant's Credit Association holds a banquet at the Allenel Hotel. The association would join with the Civic Improvement Association to form an Ann Arbor Chamber of Commerce in 1918.

The corner of State Street and North University in 1914.

The influx of cars led to concerns about their maintenance and regulation within the city. In 1910, the city government adopted the first set of traffic laws, with special provisions not covered by previous state decrees.

Walker's Livery was one of many businesses adapting to the ever more popular automobile. Abandoning the horse-drawn ways of the nineteenth century, the livery converted to car culture, becoming the Ann Arbor Taxicab and Transfer Company in 1914, shown here.

Van's Marine Band is on parade in 1916. Bringing up the rear are the Boy Scouts of America. Behind those assembled are an abstract office, the Y.M.C.A., and the Square Deal Garage.

Camp Birket, in 1917. Thomas Birket, a resident of Dexter, operated a summer camp for boys on the shore of Big Silver Lake, starting in 1912. In 1920, he deeded his 15 acres to the Y.M.C.A., which continued to run the camp.

The Washtenaw County Chapter of the Red Cross played an integral role in organizing aid for World War I. In May 1918, the same month this parade took place, the local Red Cross gathered a total of 11,064 garments to be sent to France.

Musicians from the Ehnis Marching Band, circa 1919. The band was a predecessor of the University of Michigan Band, and frequently played at UM football games.

LOOKING ONWARD

(1920–1950s)

The Machine Specialty Company Plant, located along the Huron River on North Main Street, is shown here in 1927. The company manufactured the unlikely combination of piston rings and radio equipment, on N. Main and on Wildt Street, employing about 50 men by 1925.

The Staebler Oil Company on State Street, circa 1920. The first Staebler filling station was located in the old Philip Bach mansion on Main Street. Businesses offering automobile services were on the rise in the 1920s. At the start of the decade, Ann Arbor had 15 garages, 9 auto repair shops, and 4 rental companies.

After World War I, several new churches sprang up to serve the growing community of laborers who came to work on the city's many building projects.

Liberty Meat Market, at 118 West Liberty Street, circa 1920. Sullivan's Cadillac hams are advertised as "the brand to demand."

Staebler & Sons was a prominent name in the Ann Arbor automobile business. Staebler started out in 1885 as a purveyor of bicycles and offered the first car in 1900, the Trimoto (sometimes nicknamed the "Tomato"), a three-wheeled vehicle made by the American Bicycle Company of Chicago. By the 1930s, Staebler had switched completely to automobiles. Pictured is their showroom at 119 West Washington Street, circa 1930.

The Bethlehem Church of Christ served an almost exclusively German immigrant community in Ann Arbor well into the twentieth century. Until 1916 services were conducted only in German. Gradually the church began to offer services in English, and by 1922, when this group portrait was made, even the parish school had begun to teach pupils in English. The sanctuary dates from 1895. Designed by Rasemann, an architect out of Detroit, it was built for a sum of $20,000.

In August 1927, diners at Prochnow's Dairy Lunch on Main Street were rattled from their meals by a spectacular crash. Four cars from the Interurban train had slipped their couplings and rolled down the tracks into town, finally derailing and smashing into the Farmers and Mechanics Bank. The building sustained great damage, but miraculously, no one was injured.

The Ann Arbor Daily News building, in 1936.

Interior of a men's clothing store, in 1932. Ties and bowties are *in*.

Two company vehicles advertise Drake's Sandwich Shop, at 820 East University Avenue.

Lindenschmitt, Apfel & Company, Clothiers, Hatters and Furnishers, at 209 South Main Street, in 1934.

Quarry Drug Store on North University and South State Street. A sign to the left says "New Location For Moe's Barber Shop." The building is now home to the Michigan Book and Supply Store.

Through the Works Progress Administration, many different public works facilities were built in Ann Arbor during the Great Depression. Here, WPA workers construct a band shell in West Park. The band shell still stands and continues to be a popular summer venue for concerts and other events.

The Quarry Drugstore. Upstairs, the Laura Belle Shop is holding a sale.

Soap Box Derbies were popular entertainment, and were sponsored by local groups, such as the Junior Chamber of Commerce.

During the war, the Junior Chamber of Commerce was a central organizer of relief efforts and programs for young people. The group was founded in Ann Arbor in 1935 and by 1941 it enrolled 93 members. Although it was responsible for many different kinds of community service projects, its "War Services" branch was especially active. One hundred percent of Ann Arbor "Jaycee" members participated in war services projects in the early 1940s.

The Junior Chamber of Commerce also organized events for veterans returning from the war after 1945. Shown here is a recreation event.

The Ann Arbor Police Band performs in a parade in celebration of Rededication Week 1948.

Liberty Street, 1952.

NOTES ON THE PHOTOGRAPHS

These notes, listed by page number, attempt to include all aspects known of the photographs. Each of the photographs is identified by the page number, a title or description, photographer and collection, archive, and call or box number when applicable. Although every attempt was made to collect all data, in some cases complete data may have been unavailable due to the age and condition of some of the photographs and records.

II **ANN ARBOR PANORAMA, 1890**
Bentley Historical Library, University of Michigan
HS1578

VI **RECRUITING OFFICER**
Bentley Historical Library, University of Michigan
BL001186

X **HANGSTERFER BLOCK**
Bentley Historical Library, University of Michigan
BL000817

2 **GREGORY HOUSE, 1868**
Bentley Historical Library, University of Michigan
BL000823

3 **MAIN STREET**
Bentley Historical Library, University of Michigan
BL000919

4 **FIRST PRESBYTERIAN**
Bentley Historical Library, University of Michigan
HS1675

5 **ANN STREET, 1875**
Bentley Historical Library, University of Michigan
BL000335

6 **FIRE DEPARTMENT**
Bentley Historical Library, University of Michigan
HS1660

7 **DRAKE'S SALOON**
Bentley Historical Library, University of Michigan
BL000909

8 **STATE STREET FACING NORTH**
Bentley Historical Library, University of Michigan
BL000281

9 **HURON RIVER**
Bentley Historical Library, University of Michigan
HS1600

10 **BEER DELIVERY WAGON**
Bentley Historical Library, University of Michigan
BL000902

11 **NICKELS MEAT MARKET**
Bentley Historical Library, University of Michigan
HS1596

12 **FIRST GERMAN CHURCH**
Bentley Historical Library, University of Michigan
BL000317

13 **VIEW FROM THE NORTHWEST**
Bentley Historical Library, University of Michigan
BL000017

14 **ORGAN WORKS**
Bentley Historical Library, University of Michigan
BL000302

15 **RAILROAD TRESTLE**
Bentley Historical Library, University of Michigan
HS1661

16 **SECOND COURTHOUSE**
Bentley Historical Library, University of Michigan
BL000297

17 **SEVENTH-GRADE CLASS PICTURE**
Bentley Historical Library, University of Michigan
BL001174

18 **ICEHOUSE ON HURON RIVER**
Bentley Historical Library, University of Michigan
HS1645

19 **CENTRAL MILLS**
Bentley Historical Library, University of Michigan
BL000363

20 **SKATING PARTY**
Bentley Historical Library, University of Michigan
HS1631

21 **THE GERMANIA CLUB, 1885**
Bentley Historical Library, University of Michigan
HS17012

22 **SKYLINE FROM UNIVERSITY HALL**
Bentley Historical Library, University of Michigan
HS1603

23 **UNIVERSITY HEATING PLANT**
Bentley Historical Library, University of Michigan
HS15672

24 **STATE STREET**
Bentley Historical Library, University of Michigan
HS1604

25 **GERMANIA HOTEL**
Bentley Historical Library, University of Michigan
HS1617

26 **BICYCLE CLUB**
Bentley Historical Library, University of Michigan
HS1594